# The Ju~~kebox Boys~~

## And Other Boyhood Memories

# Works by B. Ellen Gardner

*Novels*

Guardian Spirit
A Trail of Twenty Winters
The Lamplighter
Shae's Song
When Warriors Cried

*Poetry and Prose*

Finding Beauty and Other Intangibles
A Collection of Poetry and Prose

# The Jukebox Boys

## And Other Boyhood Memories

A Collection of Stories and Poetry

B. Ellen Gardner

**Cover Design:** Jacqueline E. Smith

**Models:** Landry Langford, Brock Rodgers, Gabe Rodgers, and Hudson Bridges

**Photos:** Taken at MG's of Sherman, TX

**ISBN:** 13 - 9781701677180

# Dedications

This book is lovingly dedicated to
my grandsons. You have given me more
joy than you will ever realize.

Landry

Brock

Gabe

Hudson

## A Special Dedication

To Jim, Kathy, and Dick

## Thank You

Chanel Stiggers and MG's of Sherman, TX

# A Note from the Author

I put together this collection of stories and poetry as a gift to my grandsons. As a mother of two daughters and a sister to seven other women, learning first-hand about boys and their antics has been an adventure I feel blessed to have been given the opportunity to experience.

It's been a fun journey and I look forward to the years ahead. As the years pass by far too quickly, it is with great fondness and a little bit of sorrow that I share memories of my grandsons. I know these memories will resonate with all of those who have had the privilege of watching young boys grow into gentlemen.

# Contents

**Boyhood   1**
Jukebox Boys
My Wheels
Sounds Boys Make
The ABC's of Surviving Boyhood

**Family and Pets   9**
Double Trouble
Family
Game Night
Giblets
Harley &Jett
Papa's Lap
Pickle Boy
Swimmy
The Value of a Dollar
Waterworks

**Great Outdoors   31**
Camping
Dinosaur Discovery
Nothin' Like Fishin'

**Heroes and Legends   37**
Cowboy Life
Four Little Wranglers
Little Professor Jones
Not All Heroes Wear Capes
Super Hero

## Holidays   47

Christmas Spirits
Father's Day Blessings
Father Time
I'm Thankful For
Prize Egg

## Important Things   63

God Matters
Memories of You
My Boys
Oh, Beautiful
The Best Times
Twinkling Star

## School   73

Best Teachers Ever
Handy Guy
Kid's Honor
More Than a Grade
Roof Antics
Take Care of Him
When I'm at School

## Sports   85

Billy Ray
Second Baseman and Shortstop
The Great Bambino
Varsity Basketball

## Vacations & Ventures 95
Coffee Detour
Ghost Town
The Fonzie Look

# Boyhood

Boyhood comes but once in a lifetime,
but the memories live on forever.

# Jukebox Boys

Boys are like songs on a jukebox.
They come in a variety of choices.
While some are slow and easy-going,
Others are fast and uncompromising,
Each having their own special voices.

Some songs make you want to dance,
And some bring you to tears.
Still, others share a mixture of melancholy,
Tugging away at the core of your heart,
Changing melodies throughout the years.

The songs commence life's many dances.
As the first note plays, it takes you to a day,
When times were simpler and worries were few;
And the most important thing to do,
Was let the music carry your mind away.

With a push of a button the songs personate.
Songs of happiness and sorrows unfold.
The music reflects moments in time,
The highs and the lows, the old and the new.
Memories are locked within the soul as solid gold.

# My Wheels

It started with Match Cars,
This fascination for Hot Wheels.
I rolled them through the house
Imagining they were real.

Soon, it was on to Big Wheels.
I hunkered down to ride.
Like Earnhardt, I put on my helmet.
There's no other feeling inside.

Along came a big boy's bike,
How proud I was that day.
A little shaky at first when…
Dad took the training wheels away.

I became a grand and worthy master
Riding carefree up and down the roads.
But as I grew it was on to bigger wheels.
My treasured ride was squeaky and old.

Then came Three and Four-wheelers
Dune Buggies and Go-Carts
I sailed through the world
With adventure in my heart.

A grown man now I still recall with joy,
Racing down unknown trails on my wheels.
With the wind in my hair and thrill in my veins,
I was invincible as time stood still.

# Sounds Boys Make

Oh, the sounds boys make…
Unwords like huh and duh
Or grunts like Grr and Err
Or both together grrerr, duhhuh

They screech and they shriek
and squawk and knock
They tap and flap
Or snip and snap

They belch like Shrek
With a smell just as foul
Then burp in unison
With their best pal

At the drop of a hat
They can let one rip
Proud as punch and filled with glee
Most especially when it's an SBD

# The ABC's of Surviving Boyhood

**A**lways aim for the center of the commode.

**B**rush your teeth more than once a week.

**C**hicken strips are not the only food.

**D**ream to your heart's content.

**E**gos are for politicians, not kids.

**F**loors are not hampers.

**G**randparents are your best allies.

**H**eroes live all around you.

**I** is the loneliest word.

**J**esus is the real deal.

**K**indness is always in season.

**L**istening is not just for others.

**M**oney is most valuable when it's earned.

**N**oses run so keep them clean.

**O**pen it — close it.

**P**arents have the toughest job in the world.

**Q**uit complaining and change what's wrong.

**R**espect others and expect the same for yourself.

**S**tand tall for the flag.

**T**exting is not the same as talking.

**U**se the manners your parents taught you.

**V**elcro your mouth shut when it spews cruel words.

**W**anting is not needing.

**X**boxes have nothing on cardboard boxes.

**Y**ellow snow is not for eating.

**Z**ippers are there to keep everything inside.

# Family and Pets

Family is the heart of all that is
wonderful about our world.

# Double Trouble

Born on the same day
Born of the same father and mother
Just minutes separate this duo
From one another.

This iconic, dynamic twosome
Are skilled tricksters to be sure
What wiles one doesn't think of
The other is ready to procure.

Experience is their favorite teacher
These skilled tricksters of mayhem
Quickly unfold their clever schemes
Before Dad and Mom can stop them!

Many nicknames describe the two
Lightning and Thunder, Tank and Jet
The Rock and Muscles
The Train and the Wreck.

And each day their roles may be different
On a given day one is the instigator
On another, he's cleaning up the mess
The worst days are when both play terminator.

Yet whatever trouble may follow the pair
It's safe to say that these twins of ploy
Along with confusion and utter anarchy
Brings to their family deep love and deep joy!

# Family

**F** is for family coming from both far and near.
It's wearing friendly faces along with tears.
It's festive gatherings held year after year.
It's fathers welcoming all with gusto and cheer.

**A** is for aunts with their arms open to greet,
bringing apple pies along with other tasty treats.
They tell family stories in detail and with glee,
of the ancestry and history of our family tree.

**M** is for memories we cannot sever.
It's a mosaic of descendants linked together.
It's the marriage of two souls joined forever.
It's a mother's love we will always remember.

**I** is for in-laws with love in their hearts.
It's for identical twins you can't tell apart.
It's the many inherit characteristics and marks.
The intricate history that we long to impart.

**L** is for love and a lifetime with your soulmate.
It's for little babies and the laughter they make.
It's the lineage of family and how we relate.
It's giving to life more than you take.

**Y** is for young, a new generation of promise,
brothers and sisters, husbands and wives,
Sons and daughters, who never compromise.
Retelling yesterday as seen through their eyes.

# Game Night

It's game night. I can hardly wait.
The popcorn's popped and I'm feeling great.
The family's almost ready to begin.
I can feel it in my bones. I'm going to win.

The board is ready.  The dice are cast.
We roll them to see who goes last.
No arguments from me when I'm not first.
It's the eldest syndrome, the first-born curse.

Around and around the board we go.
Where luck takes us nobody knows.
Just when I'm about to ploy my strategy.
Everyone breaks because they are hungry.

After an eternal break, we begin again.
When Dad hits big, my head spins.
When Mom gets lucky and hits a big payday,
I start to think things aren't going my way.

My brother screams when he loses his money.
My sister and I laugh 'cause we think it's funny.
Dad tells us if we don't stop the game is done.
Mom says being mean ruins all of the fun.

I tell my little brother not everyone can win.
He tells my parents to start over again.
They give my sister and me a consoling stare.
They start the game over even if it's not fair.

My sister bows out claiming game night is lame.
My dad looks at me and asks if I feel the same.
I know it's best not to say how I really feel.
"Heck no," I say. My fake smile appears real.

# Giblets

## (An Unusual Pet and Friend)

Oh, Giblets, why did you have to go?
Now I'm all alone.
Even though I know
I couldn't hold on to you forever,
It doesn't keep me from missing you so!

I found you lying in the garden all alone,
So I picked you up and said,
"I'll take you home."
When fate took you away from me,
My heart could do nothing but moan.

I know it's silly to love you so,
My strange little green friend.
You were just a simple jalapeno.
But the moment we touched
I knew I wanted to watch you grow.

There are other peppers in the garden there,
Some more plump and spicy,
For me though, no other can compare.
I will never forget you my sweet Giblets,
I close my eyes and see you everywhere!

# Harley & Jett

Jett is faster than lightening
Strong and quick like a mighty wind
He speeds throughout the house
Over and over again!

Harley is docile and subdue
Soft and gentle like a summer breeze
He finds a quiet spot close to a human
Stares into their face with persuasive pleas.

Two very loved pet terriers
One Boston and one Yorkshire
When Harley barks you don't hear a peep
Jett's howl is like the sound of a town crier.

When it comes to family the two are alike
As a member of the pack, they are top dog,
Loved and cherished by their human kinfolk,
They are forever part of the family travelogue.

# Papa's Lap

The many things I learn on Papa's lap
Are lessons filled with love and respect.
For every moment he holds me in his arms
Are moments I will never forget.

He shows me unconditional love
And how to live for each and every moment.
He shows me through the times we share
That I am a blessing and that I am important.

His lap can be anywhere or any place
In church, at a ballgame, or in his chair.
We speak of things only meaningful to us.
In joy and sadness, Papa's lap is always there.

It is the living of each and every moment
And not the things that he can give to me.
It's showing me that love is the only thing
That will remain in my heart and my memory.

When years pass by and I'm too big for Papa's lap
I will not let go of the love and bond we share.
We will continue our conversations in other ways
Until the day when one of us is no longer there.

# Pickle Boy

Some know him as the pickle boy,
A natural-born entrepreneur.
His innate charm and collective wit
Are only part of his allure.

His smile draws in the public.
His pitch is perfectly expressed.
His humor and grit enchant all.
His great products do the rest.

Day after day and week after week
The pickle boy can be seen all around.
His face and pickles are a familiar sight
In homes, in markets, and in towns.

No one can deny his dedication
Nor his ability to close a deal.
Yet it's his pride and love for his family
That make his sales pitches real.

# Swimmy

I won you at a carnival booth,
A prize I will forever cherish.
I made your home a bowl of water
And swore to never let you perish.

You lived longer than anyone expected.
And so my mom bought you a new bowl,
A larger one with more room to swim.
Your dull coloring turned bright gold.

I named you Swimmy for obvious reasons.
I watched you swim day after day.
I never dreamed, my little friend,
That someday you would go away.

You did go away I'm sad to say.
Still, you lived a year and I am told,
That for a goldfish you were quite old,
My little Swimmy, so strong and bold.

I tried to love another.
I called him your little brother.
But your brother only lived a day.
I guess I wasn't meant to have another.

Sweet little Swimmy of long ago,
I still recall your color of bright gold.
There is one thing I want you to know.
When I think of you my heart still glows.

# The Value of a Dollar

Dad ran frantically around the house searching for something. As he searched, he clearly became more and more agitated. I knew it was best to stay out of his way and just let the morning run its course. Vaguely we heard mom ask my dad what he was looking for. His keys. He couldn't find his keys.

Two minutes later he was hollering at me and my little brother. "I'll give the person who finds my keys a crisp one-dollar bill."

We went scrambling throughout the house trying to find my Dad's keys — under sofas, under tables, under laundry, in the dog's bed, and even in the refrigerator. No luck. Then, I looked over at my baby sister sitting contentedly in her playpen chewing on a squeeze toy and holding onto something else. Could it be? I doubted it, but I ran toward the playpen just the same. Low and behold, there were Dad's keys, along with his phone. I snatched up both before my baby sister could notice them gone.

"Found them!" I shouted.

Dad was elated and without blinking an eye, he handed me a crisp one-dollar bill. I waited for the next words to come out of Dad's mouth as I noted him patting his pant pockets as if searching for something. A phone perhaps? Sure enough, Dad started calling out in that chaotic voice once again.

"I'm already late and now my phone is missing."

I could wait it out and see if Dad might offer up another dollar bill, but his agitation told me that he was in no mood. Also, I needed Dad to take me to get my basketball shoes after work today. No need to upset him any further. I tapped him on the sleeve and handed him his phone. He looked at me strangely at first and then smiled.

"Thanks, Son," he said. "I owe you."

In less than five minutes Dad and my brother and I were out the door. Mom and my baby sister remained at home.

After supper that night, I politely reminded dad about the basketball shoes I needed. He frowned knowing he had to take me. He was bone-tired from work.

Seeing the despairing look on his face I said, "It can wait 'till tomorrow."

He looked at me smiling.

"You've been very thoughtful today, Son. It means a lot to me. No, we'll go tonight. I like the person you're becoming."

It made me feel good that Dad thought I was growing up. For some reason, I started to clear up the dishes for mom. Mom looked at me surprised because in my life I had never helped her with the dishes without my dad lecturing me. I smiled at Mom and she smiled back.

In ten minutes, my dad and I were on our way to the sporting good's store. Dad was in a good mood, singing and tapping the steering wheel. Soon I was singing and tapping my feet. It was a great ride to the store.

At the sporting good's store, it didn't take me long to find the shoes I wanted. Once again, Dad had a despairing look on his face. He's not too great at hiding his emotions. I asked him if something was wrong. He replied with a sad quiver in his voice.

"These shoes are a bit expensive, Son. Mind if we look for some that cost a little less?"

My heart was set on these particular shoes and I know my face showed my disappointment. I guess I'm not good at hiding my emotions either. Dad looked at me and was fully aware of my disappointment. He put his hand on my shoulder.

"I know you can't understand now, but a year from now, maybe even sooner than that, you won't even remember these shoes. You'll be thinking of something else you want. Now, let's find a pair that are less expensive. I promise they will be nice shoes."

I wanted to resort to my pouty old self but something inside of me remembered the feeling I felt on the ride tonight with my dad. It was the best feeling, like Dad and I had connected in a way we had never connected before. I tried to brave a smile, but I really wanted those shoes. I begrudgingly said.

"Sure, Dad," I said. "I understand," even though I didn't.

I did find myself a pair of shoes. They weren't the cool ones nor were they the color I wanted, but I pretended that I was happy with them. When we left the store, Dad made a stop by the ice cream store and we each got a cone. We were back to being pals again.

When we got home, the house was quiet. My brother and sister were already in bed. Dad told me to get my shower and get ready for bed myself.

As I showered, I began to think of the fun time I had with my dad tonight. He seemed like a different person, not all stressed and all. I thought of the shoes I got and the ones I really wanted. Something my dad said hit me like a ton of bricks. Something about the value of money. It suddenly dawned on me. It wasn't that Dad didn't want me to have the cool shoes, it was that he didn't have the money.

Later that night in bed, I started thinking about my dad and how hard he works. I thought of the dollar bill I took from him that morning when he was looking for his keys. I shouldn't have taken it. After all, we are a family, a team. We help each other.

The next morning when chaos struck again, I pretended I had lost my backpack. Running late again, Dad had everyone searching. I called out to anyone who would listen.

"I have a crisp one-dollar bill for the person who finds it first."

In the pretend search, my younger brother found the backpack and called out, "Found it!"

Without blinking an eye, I handed him the dollar bill Dad had given me yesterday morning. My little brother's eyes beamed. He tucked it into his pocket as if it were a million dollars. Dad patted me on the back as we walked out to the car that morning. He spoke for my ears only.

"I'm on to you, Son. I know you didn't lose your backpack. You're the most organized person I know."

I smiled but continued to pretend. "I don't know what you're talking about, Dad."

On the ride to school, I saw my little brother pull out his new dollar bill admiring it with pride. He couldn't stop smiling. I commented to my brother.

"Thanks for helping me find my backpack."

Still smiling, he said, "You're welcome."

My brother and I don't usually get along but looking at his face and seeing his smile made my heart swell. I looked at my dad. I was seeing him in a new light. I knew that these feelings wouldn't always last and that tomorrow or maybe even later on today, I would be aggravated with both my dad and little brother. For now, though, I thought of the value of a crisp one-dollar bill and the dividend I had received from paying it forward. I couldn't put a price tag on the way I felt at this moment. It was a humbling lesson in the value of a dollar.

# Waterworks

In her younger years she was a fashion statement, always dressed with utmost style. Her hair was always kempt and her smile was always bright. When she married, she created a home for her husband and herself. This home was a dream, cozy and warm. It was the kind of home you'd see in a magazine, filled with style and country charm. And then, she and her husband had the children…

*…Fast forward seven years and three children later.*

To say that life had changed for her was an understatement. Raising three children was quite a challenge, especially when two of these young children were twins. Surviving each day without injury and mishaps was a day well-accomplished. Each day, each moment, brought new and unexpected, almost unheard of, discourse. She and her husband quickly learned that parenthood was not for the faint of heart nor the weak in spirit. They came to understand that being a parent would be the toughest job they would ever do.

No day was more challenging than the days in which the family ventured an outing. Packing up three kids, putting them in their car seats without arguments, and keeping them entertained until you reached your destination would no doubt test the patience of a saint, let alone young parents.

The most challenging outings were those when one parent braved to venture out without the help of the other.

Such was the case one particular day when Mom decided to take her three darlings out. Dad was out of town for work. It was a beautiful day. The kids were cooperating. Things were running smoothly, more smoothly than usual. This should have been her first clue. Blinded by optimism, the hopeful mom took on the adventure. What could go wrong on such a beautiful day?

She packed the bags — extra clothing, wipes, and snacks. Check. She dressed the kids. No problems there. Surprisingly, there was little incident when she put them in their car seats. She was almost giddy. She pulled out of the driveway and as she drove down the road, she was singing and whistling. Sounds of joy were coming from the vehicle. Mom's heart was soaring. She loved her babies. She loved her life. A sense of confidence filled her being. Life was good.

The day brought on few challenges. In fact, the kids were so cooperative, Mom made a run through McDonalds and picked up three happy meals to reward her darlings. They would have a picnic in the park. The kids cheered and clapped their hands when she drove to the park and they saw the play equipment. The moment the kids stepped out of the car was when peace turned into mayhem.

They began fighting and running from mom. They were poking each other. Mom chased after the twins who started running toward the street. The oldest child, a girl, was sulking because she didn't get the toy in her happy meal that she wanted. Mom was completely frayed only fifteen minutes into the picnic. Her optimism was shattering. She happened to glance up to see one twin attempting to climb the highest slide on his own. Exasperated, she quickly ran after him. In the time it took her to rescue him, the other twin was feeding his happy meal to a strange dog that had wandered up upon their picnic.

"Don't touch the dog!" Mom yelled. "He could bite!"

Too late. The dog took off with the twin's chicken nuggets. The boy screamed for his food. With one twin under her arm and the other twin screaming, Mom had had it. She grabbed the screaming twin and called for the six-year-old to follow them to the car. In less than five minutes, she had the kids in their car seats, what was left of the food, and had gathered up the bags. She smelled something rank coming from one of the twins and knew he had most likely had an accident. She couldn't worry about it now. She was too spent. It could wait until they got home.

Driving home, the upheaval and chaos she was so familiar with had shown its ugly face and tainted the beautiful day. The twins were screaming. The six-year-old was poking. The gas light went on. She hoped she could make it home before she ran out of gas. Her cell phone was almost dead. And of course, her car charger was nowhere to be found. The rest of the drive home was a mass of confusion with her making threats, kids screaming, toys and food being hurled throughout the car. When she drove into the garage, she was at the end of her rope.

For a moment, she sat behind the wheel of the car and prepared herself for the remainder of the day. With courage, she opened the door to the car, got out, and put the key into her back door. The little energy she had left drained from her being. It was replaced by utter disillusionment. For what she found as she opened up the door and walked into her den was unimaginable. Her youngest twin (she would learn later) had accidentally plugged up the sink in the master bathroom with a washcloth and had left the water running. A river of water flowed throughout the house. The greater part of the damage was in the master bedroom, the hallway, and the den.

She couldn't speak. She couldn't yell. She couldn't think. She just stared for the longest time at the disaster before her. She had no clue how to deal with what faced her. In the end, it was her six-year-old that took command of the situation. She took her mom's phone and called for reinforcements. She called Mimi.

"Mimi," she said. "Mommy needs you. She's crying and I can't get her to stop."

When Mimi arrived with her other daughter, she saw her eldest daughter sitting on the carport in a state of dismay. Shock might be the better word to describe her. Without a well thought out plan, Mimi put the kids in her car and took them to her house. She left her two daughters to take care of the damage done to the house.

It would be months before Mom was able to laugh at the situation. She eventually did. She realized that in the scheme of life a little waterworks (both physically and emotionally) were low on the priority list where loved ones and family were concerned. Her children were safe and sound and happy. The house had survived and had received a new facelift in the process. Mom became mindful that the only thing in life she could predict was that the unexpected could be right around the corner.

# Great Outdoors

Boyhood and the outdoors
are inseparable.

# Camping

It's hard to pick the best part of camping.
But after a long and fun-filled day outdoors,
there's nothing like sitting around the fire
or roasting marshmallows and making S'mores.

Stories are relayed with exaggerated flair,
of heroes and legends and villains of long ago.
Scary renditions of old ghost tales are told,
and haunting voices echo as the wind blows.

Later at night when the campfire fades
into a soft amber glow and smoldering heap,
we let our imaginations run away with us;
as the creatures of the night disturb our sleep.

As we wait for sleep, shadows of the night
become grotesque visions of evil obscurities.
Maybe it's Big Foot or the spirit of an outlaw.
We clutch tight to each other for security.

We awake to the dawn of a new adventure
and climb out of our tents to see the sunrise.
Having escaped the night of ghoulish invasions,
our courage soars to face a new day of surprises.

# Dinosaur Find

We take out our picks, shovels, and tools
those archeologists use to search the unknown.
There's no telling what treasures we will discover,
gold, silver, jewels, rocks, or even lost bones.

Mom packs us a snack and fills up our thermos.
Though it's a bit cold outside the sun is bright.
We start just a few feet from the back door,
never getting too far from mom's sight.

As we dig, we plan what we will do
when we are rewarded for our endeavors.
A great find will make us rich and famous.
Our names will go down in history forever.

It doesn't take long until we hit something hard.
Our hands dig fast as our spirits soar.
We see a long bone and stare with astonishment.
Certain we have found the remains of a dinosaur.

A T-Rex? A Brontosaurus? We can't be sure.
We are only sure that we've found something big.
We carry the bones like fragile glass to the house,
where we proudly show Mom our infamous dig.

She smiles with a kindness only moms can show
and brings us a container to place our find.
She is proud of us and our dinosaur discovery,
and our contribution to the history of mankind.

# Nothin' Like Fishin'

Oh, there's nothin' like fishin'
outside in the fresh air of nature.
Just me and my fishing rod,
my tackle box, and lures.

I step near the edge of the water
and cast out my line.
Patiently, I wait for a bite,
a tug, a nibble, a sign.

I'm as carefree as the pesky insects
that whirr and swarm all around.
Contented, I'm not in a hurry,
absorbed in nature's sounds.

All of a sudden my line starts to pull.
I reel in my catch with excitement and grit.
It's a beauty to be sure, must be a three-footer.
After inspecting it, three inches is a better fit.

# Heroes and Legends

The greatest heroes are those
who remain nameless.

# The Cowboy Life

There is no life like the cowboy life,
Rugged, honest, and real.
The cowboy needs little to make him content,
Just his horse, his rope, a good meal.

He wakes up at dawn with the same goals,
To keep the promises he's made.
Loyal to his God, his family, and his heart,
His duty rarely falters or fades.

At the end of a hard day of work,
The cowboy takes off his hat and boots.
He gives his burdens to the Lord above,
Thanking Him for his life and his cowboy roots.

Some may view the cowboy's life as unrefined,
While others may romanticize the role.
Recalling the many heroes of the Old West,
Whose tales are embedded within history's soul.

# Four Young Wranglers

Four young wranglers sat on a fence at the end of a long day of work waiting for their pay. The boss man asked each one individually what they had learned that day.

The oldest and most experienced wrangler told the boss man that he worked all day trying to gentle the new filly and he thought she had finally warmed up to him.

The boss man and the first wrangler went to the stalls. Sure enough, the filly was calmer and had taken a liking to the young wrangler.

The boss man was more than impressed and he gave the wrangler his pay for the day.

The second wrangler told the boss man that he thought he had finally learned to master a knot.

"Show me," the boss man said.

In less than a minute the knot was formed. The boss man nodded and gave him his daily pay.

The third wrangler told the boss man that his day was spent mending the fence. He showed the boss how he had single-handedly repaired the fence so that it stood sturdier than it had ever been.

The boss man checked out the third wrangler's work and he didn't think he could have done any better. He smiled and patted him on the back and told him he had done a fine job. He gave him his daily wages.

The last and tiniest wrangler sat dismayed on the fence looking downhearted as the boss man asked him what he had learned today.

He told the boss man that he didn't do anything as amazing as the other wranglers. He was still afraid of the new filly. He still couldn't make a knot. He tried to help mend the fence but was chased off because he was causing more problems than he was helping. He told the boss man he guessed he didn't really learn much today, at least not anything worth getting paid for.

The boss man looked at him warmly. "Surely, there is something that you learned today. You know, we learned from our failures as well as our successes."

The little wrangler thought and thought and thought. After a long time of consideration, he gave the boss man a broad smile.

"There is one thing I learned today," he said proudly.

"Well, what is it?" the boss man asked.

"Well, Sir," he said. "I learned never to pee into the wind."

The boss man chuckled and handed the littlest wrangler his daily pay. He walked away still chuckling. A lesson learned is a lessoned learned.

# Little Professor Jones

There's a new hero in town.
He wears a brown fedora hat.
He's not your usual hero,
He's more debonair than that.

Fighting evil and destruction,
He stands just thirty-three inches small.
But don't mistake his size for weakness.
He's tough and fearless and filled with awe.

His whip is his best-known weapon,
Along with his satchel filled with tools.
Educated in the school of hard knocks,
His enemies know he's no fool.

He's especially dangerous when he wears
His most lethal weapon of all.
This hidden-in-plain-sight line of defense,
Has forced the most powerful despots to fall.

What's this weapon you want to know?
It's the fingerprint of his appeal.
For when little Professor Jones smiles,
His enemies' fates are forever sealed.

# Not All Heroes Wear Capes

Not all heroes wear capes,
This is true.
Some are disguised in uniforms,
Some white, some red, some blue.

Nurses and doctors and paramedics
Serve us with the greatest aptitude,
Giving of themselves and sacrificing time,
Often with little or no gratitude.

Firemen and Police give us order.
No situation is too risky or too fast.
Every day they put their lives on the line,
Letting nothing interfere with their task.

Army, Navy, Marines, Air Force, Coast Guard,
And National Guard all serve to protect.
They sacrifice their homes, families, and lives,
For love of country, honor, and respect.

Heroes are everywhere, silent and unknown.
Some live next door, even in your own home.
They give of themselves with no plan or concern.
True heroes are defined by the honor they own.

# Super Hero

He dashes through the house fighting crime,
Wearing a mask and a cape as his cover.
No one knows the identity of this hero,
Though he looks suspiciously like my brother.

He jumps from chair to chair,
This unidentified master of disguise.
Battling evil and injustice at every juncture,
His actions are spontaneous and often unwise.

Sometimes his plights bring hits and misses,
An unfortunate component of his duty.
His landings might find him flat on his face.
Worse yet, an undignified plunge on his booty.

He would never admit defeat,
Nor would his tears ever get in the way.
When trials and tribulations befall him,
He packs away his cover to fight on a new day.

Tomorrow his cover might be a cape and mask,
Or a sword with the power to conquer his enemy.
It might be the snap of a powerful whip,
That strengthens his cause and hides his identity.

Oh, heroes are found in all parts of the world,
In cities, in fast cars, even in super domes.
Yet, none are braver than the small hero,
Who sleeps and fights crime in our home.

# Holidays

Holidays are get-togethers with
family and friends creating
lasting memories.

# Christmas Spirits

I will always remember the Christmas Eve
when I was a very small boy and I first began to
doubt the wisdom of my parents. The air
outside was frosty and bitter cold, but inside
our family's small home, it was Christmas
perfect. Dad had the fire steadily burning in the
fireplace. The stockings were hung with each
of our names ready for Santa to come and fill
them.

Mom's sugar cookies filled the entire house
with their delicious aroma. The tree lights
sparkled and the beautifully wrapped packages
below it shone magically underneath the lights'
glow. My brother and I were waiting for
Mom's cookies to finish baking so that we
could put some on a plate for Santa, along with
a glass of Dad's special eggnog. My heart
pounded with anticipation — filled to the rim
with joy.

There was nothing that could put a blemish on
such joy! Nothing! But then, my little brother
asked my dad a serious question. It was a
question even I, as the eldest, had never dared
to ask my parents though many times I had
wondered about the answer. Dad looked at my
little brother with both anxiousness and doubt.
Dad was clearly taken aback.

"Dad," my little brother asked. "Does Santa
have a key to our house?"

"Why no, Son," my dad said. "He doesn't need one. He comes down the chimney."

As soon as my dad said the words my brother looked at the fire burning in the fireplace and then he looked back at Dad. The doubt in my little brother's eyes was painfully obvious. Santa would be destroyed by the fire burning. Dad saw immediately his mistake. He reassured my brother.

"Don't worry, Son. Santa has a special suit, a fireproof suit."

I chimed in trying to clear my brother's concerns. "He has magic tricks that even grown-ups don't know about. Santa will be fine. He's been dealing with chimneys for years."

Dad looked at me and smiled. "Your brother is right. Now, don't worry, Son. Santa will find a way to get into the house."

"Just the same," I chimed in. "Can't we put a key under the matt at the front door?"

My dad nodded and said, "Sure, we can."

My brother seemed satisfied. Then he looked at the security alarm. Dad understood what was going on in his five-year-old head.

"I won't set the alarm tonight."

My little brother smiled, pleased with Dad's thoughtfulness. He went about his play. Soon, Mom had finished baking her cookies and we laid out a plate for Santa with a glass of Dad's traditional eggnog. It was almost time for the children to go to bed. Mom tucked us in our beds and kissed us goodnight.

"Sleep tight my boys so the magic can begin."

When she left, I laid in my bed feeling warm and cozy, reeling with eagerness about Santa's visit. My little brother was asleep almost the moment his head hit the pillow. He had a smile as big as Texas on his face. Sleep for me wasn't coming easily. Thoughts of Santa and Christmas and presents kept reeling in my head. A sudden thought brought terror to my spirit. I sprang up from my bed.

I knew that my dad put rum in his special eggnog. I thought of Santa. I didn't think it was wise for Santa to drink and drive. He might miss a house or have some kind of mishap in the sky and not be able to finish his Christmas around the world journey. And it would all be my parents' fault. I began to devise a plan to rectify the problem.

Late that night when all was quiet and still, I crept out of my bedroom and into the living room where the tree nestled beautifully in the corner and Santa's treats were there still awaiting his arrival. I sighed in relief. I wasn't too late! Santa hadn't come yet.

I went to the refrigerator and was once again stuck with a pang of fear. There was no fresh milk in the refrigerator. I couldn't exchange the eggnog with milk. Near tears, another solution came to my mind. I went to the drawer where my mom keeps a notepad and pens. I took a piece of paper and transcribed a note for Santa.

*Dear Santa,*

*My dad fixed you his favorite eggnog for a treat on your journey. Santa, he mixed the eggnog with spirits and I was afraid you wouldn't know. I don't want anything to put you in danger or delay your journey. Even Santa should not drink and drive. I decided to drink it myself instead of wasting good eggnog.*

*P.S: I also ate the cookies just in case my mom put rum in her cookies, too. They work as a team.*

*I love you, Santa. Merry Christmas*

I decided to wait and see if I might get a glimpse of Santa. I sat next to the tree and watched it thinking how much different it looked in the dark. That was the last thing I remembered.

In the wee hours of the morning, my parents found me snoring contentedly underneath the Christmas tree. I never felt it when Dad lifted me up and carried me back to my bed. I only know that when I awoke the next morning, my head was splitting from the spirits of the drink. It had all been worth it though. I had saved Christmas.

# Father's Day Blessings
## (Through Grandma's Eyes)

All Children are blessings born with purpose.
While all babies are miracles to behold and
marvel over, those born under special
circumstances bring to light the true miracle a
baby really is. Our miracle was twofold, twins,
born on Father's Day. So begins the magic of my
story.

Strange how things come about. The nursery for
the twins had just been painted the day before my
daughter went into labor. The cribs were up and
the drawers were filled with sweet clothes to dress
our precious boys in. There were two of
everything and we couldn't be more excited. Of
course, there was still plenty to do, but there was
time. The boys wouldn't be arriving for two
months. Now we just had to wait patiently for
our blessings to come into the world.

Our blessings and God had other plans.

My daughter came to me the very night the
nursery had been painted saying that she and my
son-in-law were going to the ER. Something
wasn't right. They wanted to have things checked
out. My husband and I stayed with their three-
year-old while they went. I was concerned but
not overly.

Several hours later, I received the call that the doctors and nurses at our local hospital were doing everything they could to keep the twins from arriving early. My concern was heightened. My son-in-law's mother called me and said she was going to the hospital and asked me to go with her. My husband took over babysitting duties.

When we arrived at the hospital, things began to move very quickly. We were hopeful that the medical people could prolong the births, even if only for a few weeks. The longer the babies remained in the womb, the greater their chances were of being born healthy and surviving. I looked at our twins' other grandmother. She took my hand. She was a rock. Definitely, a woman to have in your corner during a crisis.

Just when we thought we were out of the woods, my daughter went into labor. Before I knew what was happening, she was put in an ambulance. My son-in-law, his mom, and I were in his truck following it. The ambulance was taking my daughter to a larger hospital where they dealt on a daily basis with premature births. It housed a renowned NICU (neonatal intensive care unit) Center. I didn't dare look at the speed we were going. I only know that it was fast.

Just minutes from the hospital, my son-in-law realized that he was driving on fumes. We had to stop to get gas or we wouldn't get to the hospital. The ambulance had arrived at the hospital and my daughter was already in the delivery room when we pulled into the parking lot. Inside the hospital, my son-in-law was hoisted into protective clothing and quickly taken to the room where my daughter was ready to deliver. He got there just in time to see their first son's head move from out of the birth canal. Miracle number one. Minutes later their second son was born. Miracle number two. Happy Father's Day!

Outside of the delivery room awaited two anxious grandmothers, and soon to arrive were two anxious grandfathers. Our three-year-old was now in the capable hands of her aunt. All was going well, but worry set in when news of the births was delayed to those waiting outside. We joked and teased outside, telling the story of following the ambulance and almost running out of gas. You can't make this stuff up. Deep down, we were concerned. Were our babies all right? Was my daughter?

Sometime later, a proud dad came out of the delivery room. The boys were fine, but the road to complete recovery would be long. They both weighed less than three pounds. They literally fit in their father's hand. There were complications, as well. It would be weeks of intense care before the boys were able to go home. It was a period of uncertainty, and it put life into perspective.

There were ventilators, monitors, blood procedures, and surgeries, along with the day to day, hour to hour, minute to minute care. The unit that cared for our twins was, for lack of a better word, phenomenal. No words can describe the facilities. The staff can best be described as angels on earth. They were with our boys throughout the entire ordeal. The twins, our God-given angels, fought as courageously as did the staff and family who cared for them. Yet none fought as diligently as did their parents, watching with pain and hope as their babies went through ordeal after ordeal.

The most difficult part was the unknown and trusting strangers to love the boys as much as their family did. Those who loved them cried along with my daughter and son-in-law as they left their sons each night, entrusting them to the care of others. They were worn from worry and uncertainty, knowing that even if they survived, there could be complications up the road. Yet, as each day passed and the boys grew strong and healthy, our deep concern began to turn into great relief. We were able to share our joy and love for the newest members of our family. God had seen them through.

During this time period, my daughter and son-in-law became close to the other parents whose babies were in the unit. It was a bond they shared, one no one but those who had been through such an ordeal might understand. Not all of the hopeful parents would have our happy ending. Some were forced to face the tragedy of losing a child. Their precious baby wouldn't be coming home.

Seven weeks after their births, the oldest twin was able to make the journey home. Leaving his younger brother each day was agonizing for my daughter and son-in-law. They never gave up hope, believing he had survived so far, he would live a long and productive life. One week after his brother, after many tears and prayers, the youngest twin got to go home. It was a celebration of life and love.

*Postscript:* The birth of our twins was many years ago and much of that time is a blur to everyone involved. What we took away from it is the power of love, faith, and trust in others, most especially in God. There was one particular moment that occurred a week or so after the boys were born. It's a memory I will never forget.

I was visiting the NICU to see the boys. I came upon my son-in-law sitting in a rocker holding one of his sons. To this day, I'm not sure which boy it was. I only remember being completely taken aback by the expression of love I had happened upon. I saw a father holding his tiny son on his chest protecting and shielding him with a tenderness that matched his strength. My grandson was so small, so vulnerable, but his father's hand was securely placed across his back.

Knowing this man as I do, I knew instantly that I had come upon an intimate moment. It was one of reverence and love. The image is engrained in my heart forever. The father of my grandson was holding his son in his arms with absolute faith and humility, praying. I saw him wipe tears away a time or two. It was a blessed moment witnessing a father praying to the Almighty Father. I knew without a doubt that as my son-in-law was holding his son, God was holding him.

# Father Time

## (Christmas Pageant Review)

*December Review:* Only six years old he had the lead role in the Christmas Pageant — Father Time. Dressed in a long rob of gold and sporting a long, white beard, this young thespian became the part. In almost every scene he never missed a line, nor a beat. Before the night was over, the audience knew the direction this little actor would go.

He wooed the crowd with his articulation and his ability to know exactly how to win the hearts of those he entertained. He knew when to smile and when to turn and when to put on the charm. In an hour's time, the gathering was mesmerized, clapping wholeheartedly for his performance.

Few will remember what the play was about but only that this small wonder kept them captivated. They cheered for him later at the casting party consisting of cookies and punch. His performance noted the beginning of the upcoming holiday season with joy and festive merriment. No doubt this talented, upcoming star will entertain the theatric world for years and years to come.

Review by Mary Holiday

# I'm Thankful for...

There are many wonderful people
I'm thankful for today.
I won't begin to list them all.
I'd overlook someone anyway.

So I'll just give a big shout out
To everyone I know.
Thanks for coming into my life
And watching me as I grow.

Thanks to everyone and anyone
Who came today and made food for my belly.
I've been waiting patiently for days to taste
Homemade rolls filled with cranberry jelly.

And mashed potatoes, green beans, and corn
Along with special treats made just for me;
A plump round turkey roasting in the oven
To eat with baked cheese and macaroni.

I know Thanksgiving isn't just a day
For pumpkin pie and chocolate cake.
It's a day of celebrating family and friends
And holding on to the memories we make.

On a day when food is the center of attention
And fall décors and smells fill the air;
The heart of Thanksgiving is those you are with
It's time spent together and the love you share.

# Prize Egg

Oh, the treasured prized-egg pursuit,
The great excitement on Easter Day,
When Uncle Buddy gives the first clue
That will send us on our way.

Inside the hollow plastic egg,
Lies one crisp Ben Franklin.
Our hearts are eager, our eyes beg,
To spy the allusive prize and win.

We search in crannies high and low
Following the clues, we find along the way.
They lead us to treetops and creeks below.
Only Uncle Buddy knows and will not say.

Few will make it to the end of the chase,
For it leads them far from its start.
Only the die-hard hunters will last the race.
For to win is engraved within their hearts.

Hour after hour and clue after clue.
The diligent hunters search with true grit.
When at last the time is through,
Hearing someone yell, "I found it!"

Egg hunts remain tradition year to year.
Eager children searching for the prizes inside.
Yet none are celebrated with more cheer,
Than the prize egg that Uncle Buddy hides.

# Important Things

The important things in life carry us
through our storms bringing us
peace and joy along the way.

# God Matters

I picked up my six-year-old son from my mom's house. He had a serious look on his face as if he were confused and a little bit sad. I questioned him.

"Honey, is something wrong?"

"It's not me, it's Mimi. I don't think she knows who God is. She thinks God is water. She said he doesn't matter."

"That's a very odd thing to say. Where did you get this idea? Of course, God matters to Mimi."

"She told me that when God gets hot, He disappears and floats up into the sky."

I began to wonder about what my son had said and thought that my mom must have told him the story of when Jesus walked on water, or maybe about the flood. This might explain the water and the anger God felt toward mankind.

Later that night after my son fell asleep, I called my mom and told her what he had said earlier. She was puzzled but in a few minutes, she began laughing.

"I think I know his confusion," my mom said. "Today I was boiling water to make some tea. He was fascinated by the steam that came from the tea kettle and more fascinated when it whistled.  In conversation, I told him that when water gets very hot it boils and turns into steam."

"Yea," I said to my mom.  "What does this have to do with God?"

"He was curious as to how water from the sink could become so hot it would make steam," my mom continued.  "I explained to him that the heat from the burner caused it to do so.  I then went to the freezer and took out a piece of ice.  I told him that ice was once water, as well. To make the water turn to ice, it had to get really cold in order to make it freeze.

"I told him that when I was young my mom used the analogy of water to explain the Holy Trinity (God) to me.  She said that God was three persons in one God, just as water is three forms of matter (liquid, solid, or gas).  I told him that water is always water no matter what form it's in, just as God is always God no matter what form he takes on (Father, Son, or Holy Spirit).

I chuckled.  "Mom, the next time you use an analogy to explain God to a six-year-old, make sure he understands the concept of the analogy. He has no clue what matter is."

"He will someday," my mom assured.  "He will also understand just how much God matters."

# Memories of You

From the first day, I held you,
You made my world brighter,
Innocent and completely dependent
On the big people.
I still cry at the thought of that day,
My sweet little grandson.
Memories of me holding you will never go away.

Your smell, your smile, your soft gurgles,
The way your eyes followed my voice,
My heart was so filled with love for you.
When you laughed, I laughed.
I didn't know my love for you could grow,
But it did and it still does.
Memories of you strengthen my spirit.

As you grew, so did my love for you.
I celebrated you crawling, eating, your first steps.
I couldn't keep up with all you were discovering.
The months and years went flying by.
You were becoming independent and strong.
I cheered you on as you accomplished new feats.
Memories of pride can never be forgotten.

Though not a man yet, you're no longer a boy,
I watch you with wonder as you grow.
Taking two steps forward and one step back.
Know that mistakes are part of learning.
Never forget how much you are loved.
I am but a whisper away from you.
Memories of you keep me forever near.

# My Boys

There is a special wonder about you,
Living blessings sent to the world to bring it joy.
Your unique lights shine from your hearts.
You've brought so much love to me, my boys.

What makes you special are the very ways,
That makes you different from everyone else;
Your caring natures and your contagious spirits,
The remarkable ways you know yourselves.

Be proud of the boys you are inside.
Stand tall when others bring you down.
Someday you'll grow up to be men.
But for today, be happy and enjoy now.

I cannot keep up with your many changes.
As I watch you grow from day to year,
I realize time is slipping away from me.
I wonder, my boys, if you see my tears.

In the near future, in the blink of an eye,
You'll be the men God envisioned you to be.
You'll be your own person, mature adults.
I pray, my sweet boys, that you remember me.

# Oh, Beautiful

There is nothing more beautiful
Then seeing the world through children's eyes.
It's like seeing the world for the first time.
The wonder, the awe, the oceans, the skies.

Their faces tell the wonder of everyday worlds,
Every day, yes, but glorious just the same.
The mountains that have stood the face of time.
The lands that hold secrets of glory and fame.

Where does the marvel begin and will it end?
The tantalizing soft rains that settle on the land,
The details of the beauty of sunrises and sunsets,
Painted in the massive sky by God's own hand.

A child knows and appreciates the glory of it all.
They need no excuses to hold onto its grandeur
In their eyes, the world is a gift for us to behold,
A boundless vision designed by our Creator.

Oh, beautiful world for all eyes to see.
Oh splendid miracle let all souls rejuvenate
And bond with the past, present, and future,
To a land like our spirits is free and infinite.

# The Best Times

It's true that the best times are those times
unplanned with only a penny in your pocket. The
key component is having those you love beside
you.

You kick back and watch a flick on TV.
You play a game you've played a hundred times
before. You build a fort made of blankets and
chairs. You sail away on far seas using a sofa as
your boat.

You hide in a secret place where you're sure you
can't be found but your giggling gives you away.
You bury a secret treasure and map out your
route conquering pirates and bad guys along the
way.

You are a superhero using a towel as your cape
solving crimes and bringing justice to a terrified
world. And at the end of the day, you rest in
your bed which serves as the captain's seat of the
latest space cruise ship.

You plot your next adventure and let your
imagination take you to places you've never been.
You close your eyes and dream up ways to bring
balance to the chaos in the Universe.

Soon you are fast asleep, rejuvenating yourself for
tomorrow. What will it bring? No one knows.
The only thing for certain is that it will be yours
to create, yours to believe, yours to dream. For
you are the pilot of your destiny.

# Twinkling Star

You are the twinkling star that fills my night.
A loving remembrance that there is more,
More splendor, more joy, more love,
My heart can't express how I long to adore,
The breathless wonder of your very sight.

You are a beautiful song that plays in me.
No sorrow or pain can take away the joy,
That I will feel when you are in my arms.
No separation, not even death, can destroy,
The miracle of loving you for eternity.

Look down on those who love you dear.
Keep us walking near the very breath of you.
Oh, Twinkling Star, your tiny spirit fills my cup.
Our cries for you fall softly like morning dew.
Only your light of love can wash away our tears.

# School

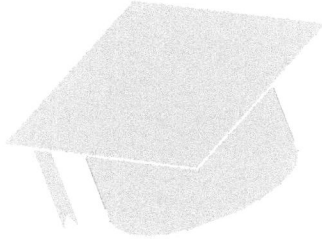

School is far more than learning
history and math. In our
every day experiences,
we discover who we
really are.

# Best Teachers Ever

The best teachers I knew taught me every day,
From sunup to sundown and even while I played.
They taught me all the things I needed to know,
And cared for my spirit as they watched me grow.

They made their share of mistakes along the way.
Despite their flaws, I learned each and every day.
Like never to give up just because you fight,
And learn it's not important to always be right.

They taught me that love is unconditional.
Their faith and trust in me made my heart full.
My life was built on a foundation based on love,
And that I am only subservient to God above.

They taught me by example to get up every day,
To face the world and let nothing get in my way.
I learned that being lost is often where life starts.
I learned that self-searching is good for the heart.

My parents are not perfect nor do they know all.
They'd be the first to ask for help when they fall.
Still, when I'm a man and far from their care,
I will never forget that they were always there.

You see, genuine love for another soul,
Is far more precious than a treasure of gold.
The unconditional love my parents gave me,
Is a gift I will hold in my heart for eternity.

My first teachers, the first to hold my hand,
Had little clue of how to handle sinking sand;
Or how to mold a rash boy into a fearless man,
Or when to let him go to make his own stand.

# Handy Guy

I'm a handy guy to have around,
When things get broken, I'll fix it fast.
I'm the fellow that will get the job done.
My rates are cheap and I'll make it last.

I like to see how objects work,
So I take them apart and look inside.
Then I put them back together again,
By using my memory as a guide.

There's not much I can't put together.
If I fail once, I just keep on striving.
If I can't fix it, I'll find someone who can.
The key to success is to never stop trying.

My mind is always thinking of new ideas,
Ways to take something old and make it new.
My brain is like a faucet that never stops running.
I never know what creation my mind will brew.

So, if you're in the market for a helpful type,
A guy to fix, or build, or create something cool.
I promise to be reliable and not disappoint.
On the job training is my type of school.

# Kid's Honor

Yes, I took out the trash.
I picked up my room.
I did my homework.
It's in my bag.
Kid's Honor!

I apologized to my brother.
I smiled at my sister.
I fed and watered the dog.
I even took him outside.
Kid's Honor!

I scraped the mud off my shoes.
I threw away my empty cans.
I never watched anything bad on TV.
I only watched what you told me I could.
Kid's Honor!

What?
Did I hide my failing math test from you?
Is that something you think I would do?
Do you really think I'd do something like that?
No, I didn't hide it.
Kid's Honor!

As I lie in my room grounded for eternity.
I wonder why my parents didn't believe me.
Did they find my wadded up test under my bed?
The dog put it there.
Kid's Honor!

# More Than a Grade

I'm more than a number in a line.
I'm more than a grade printed up on a page.
I'm more than a badge sewn on a jacket.
I'm more than a plaque with my name engraved.

I'm more than a stat on a roster.
I'm more than a title of prominence.
I'm more than a score on a scoreboard.
I'm more than dollars and cents.

Please don't measure me by worldly standards.
Measure me by me alone and what I am inside.
Measure me by what my achievements represent,
by how I gave my heart and how hard I tried.

I may not have an inscribed sign, but I was there.
I may not be number one, but I did my best.
I may not letter in a sport, but I played.
I may not make high marks, but I took the test.

I may not be tops to all, but I am to those I love.
I may not win the game, but I will give my all.
I may not be rich fiscally, but I'm rich in spirit.
I may not be the star, but I will always stand tall.

Let me grow in my heart and my dreams.
Let me learn from my mistakes and triumphs.
I am young and I have years to develop
Into a man of integrity and self-reliance.

# Roof Antics

The antics of young boys can be summed up into one word — unpredictable!

One bright day when boredom set in, four very well brought up young men decided to test fate. They had gone to their school just a few blocks from their neighborhood to shoot baskets. As they clowned around on the basketball court their ball got away from them. Somehow (hmmm) it ended up on the roof. One eager boy took the matter into his own hands.

"I'll get it," he shouted as he proceeded to climb up a pole on the side of the school. Soon he was standing on the roof. "You should come up here, too. It's really cool."

All of the boys knew their boundaries well. They knew what their parents would do if they ever found out they were climbing on the school roof. Still, the impulse was there and the thought already in their heads. Besides, one of their friends was already on the roof. They couldn't leave him up there alone.

Soon all four boys were on the roof exploring the top of the building. They came to the ledge and they decided to do what boys do best. They had a contest to see who could pee the furthest. Of course, they thought the contest was hilarious. They were laughing and carrying on and didn't see a truck pull up next to the school. When they did, one of the boys realized that it was his father. The boys decided to lie down on the roof. Maybe he wouldn't see them. No such luck. This dad wasn't going anywhere. He just sat in his truck waiting for them. They had no other choice but to climb down from the roof.

They had no doubt that they were in deep trouble. The boy's dad didn't look happy and he was good friends with all of the other boys' dads. Expecting a long lecture and maybe even calls to the other dads, they were surprised when the boy's dad said nothing.

Dad took all four boys to his house. When they went inside, he made the boys some hot dogs while the boys poured their drinks. They sat around the table anxiously awaiting their just punishment. The expected scolding never came. The wise father did, however, say something peculiar.

"You live and you learn. Now, what have you learned?"

Then, he left the four boys to ponder the situation. They looked at each other confused. Were they in trouble or were they in the clear? Would he call the other boys' parents or was this it? The uncertainty was eating at them, but they made a vow not to say anything to the other boys' parents unless they absolutely had to.

Weeks went by and no calls were made (that they knew of). No punishment was given (except for the inner turmoil that gnawed at them). They were uneasy whenever they would see a teacher or when the principal looked at them strangely (more strangely than usual). Every day they expected the storm to arrive. It never came.

The years moved on and so did the boys. It's safe to say that the experience was one the boys would not likely forget. The anguish of not knowing what would happen was a far greater punishment than restriction or a spanking would have been. The boys had been left to ponder what they had learned.

They had been given a punishment they didn't know they had received. Using love and logic, a wise dad knew the thoughts and the possible scenarios the boys would conjure up in their minds would be far worse than any punishment he could ever give them.

He knew all too well. He was a boy once, too.

# Take Care of Him

I dropped my sweet boy off at school.
I watched him walk slowly inside.
He looked so small and helpless,
My heart broke down and cried.

I told his teacher yesterday
That he likes lots of smiles.
Because he is so quiet and shy,
Smiles might ease his fears for a while.

He's always been a mama's boy,
For that, I apologize.
He's never been away from me,
Just a shadow by my side.

If he should get homesick today,
Or if he cries or gets lonely,
I put my hanky in his backpack.
He says it smells like me.

Be patient with us for a while.
It's going to take some time I know,
To adjust to this new phase in our lives,
Please give us room to grow.

# When I'm at School
## (Message from a Six-year Old)

I know more than I did when I was five, but I still have a lot to learn. I need constant reminding to do what I should do.

I can do the hard stuff like tie my shoes, but I need practice.

Reading is hard. Remember I'm new at this.

I still need hugs even though I say I don't.

The smell of Mom makes me feel safe when she's away. I close my eyes and see her there.

I want to be like my big brother. He's the best.

My dad is the smartest person in the world. He knows everything.

I really like school, even when I say I don't.

When I get in trouble I really feel bad inside.

When I don't talk, it's because I'm afraid to make a mistake.

I miss you (family) when I'm at school.

I don't need everything I want, even when I throw a fit. I want you to spend time with me not money.

At school, I can make kid decisions and not adult ones. Remember, I'm only six.

# Sports

Much of life's problems are solved
with the aid of a ball and the
support of a team.

# Billy Ray

He was proud of his mullet.
It added to his charm and appeal.
"Let's go, Billy Ray," the crowd roared
As he stood on the plate and clicked his heels.

He didn't let his good looks go to his head.
On the field, he was a beast with long hair.
He was a player his teammates could count on
To deliver a hit that could go anywhere.

He held his bat with the grip of a pro
Standing at home with confidence and dash.
Only ten years old he focused on the ball
Not a touch of a breeze to affect his blast.

The pitcher's first pitch was a speedy high ball
Knowing high balls were what he liked best.
But Billy kept his cool and let it slide by.
His patience and wit at the plate were his crests.

A tie ballgame he wouldn't let pride interfere.
The crowd cheered his name over and over again.
He waited with fortitude for just the right pitch,
To deliver the play that would bring the win.

The glare from the sun nor the heat of the day
Could stifle Billy's charm or his ability to beguile.
As the next pitch was cast his bat said it all.
He trotted all the bases in true Billy Ray style.

# Second Baseman & Shortstop

It was the first round of the state All-Stars
T-Ball championship. The players on the field
were assigned their spots. For some, their
positions weren't the usual ones they had played
throughout the season. The teams weren't the
regular season teams. This brought on some
confusion to the young five and six-year-old
players. Such was the case of the Second
Baseman and the Shortstop. They had to go by
what their coaches told them in the few practices
they had had and by good old intuition. When
the first batter hit, the players on the field were
baseball ready.

As the game progressed the second baseman
became more and more agitated with the
shortstop because he kept making the plays he
should have been making. This was not only
posing some confusion, but it was also interfering
with basic plays and giving the opposing team
unnecessary opportunities. Several innings into
the game, the second baseman confronted the
shortstop.

SECOND BASEMAN: Quit taking my plays.

He then drew an imaginary line and gave the shortstop instructions.

SECOND BASEMAN: If the ball comes on that side of the line (*he pointed to the traditional shortstop area*), it's yours. If it comes on this side of the line (*the traditional second base area*) it's mine. Now, quit taking my plays!

The little shortstop began to pout. He ran to the coach.

SHORTSTOP: Second Baseman is being mean. He says I'm not playing good.

The coach confronted the second baseman.

COACH: Shortstop says you're being mean and telling him he's not good. Is this true?

SECOND BASEMAN: I didn't say he wasn't good. I said he keeps doing it wrong.

COACH: Be patient with him. He's never played shortstop before. He's just learning.

The second baseman looked at his coach with little patience for the shortstop.

SECOND BASEMAN: Well, I've never played second base before either, but I know not to make his plays. Don't worry. I'll be nice to him after we win the game.

The coach just shook his head and walked away. He couldn't argue with the logic and determination of the young second baseman.

# The Great Bambino

He stands like a giant threat upon the mound.
His stare cuts through every batter's nerve.
His stance is steady as he pitches the ball.
Bambino's first strike is a flawless curve.

Known as Bambino on the Little League circuit
Most batters have little clue as to this power drill.
They soon learn that number three's arsenal
Is speed and accuracy and untouchable skill.

Bambino is branded as a triple threat.
While his pitching astonishes even the best.
He's also a steamroller at the plate,
As homerun after homerun can attest.

Playing cleanup has become his calling card.
His powerful bat has quieted many teams.
When Bambino walks to the plate with his bat,
The opponents fall apart at the seams.

His presence as a third baseman is boss
Sharing the spotlight with infamous names.
Greats like Beltre and Chipper and Robinson
The young leaguer is forming his fame.

Yet what makes Bambino the heart of a team
Is not his pitching, batting, or fielding.
It's his love for the game and his fortitude.
Bambino's strong character is unyielding.

# Varsity Basketball

Coach called the young freshman into his office and sat him down. He looked at him pointedly.

COACH: Son, you have two options. You can be Top Dog on the JV 2 Basketball team, or...

FRESHMAN: Or?

COACH: Or, I think you would make a great manager because what you lack in skill you make up with enthusiasm.

The young freshman thought about the coach's words. In his earlier years, he had tried to play traditional sports. When he was in Kindergarten, his parents put him on a pee-wee baseball team. He was more interested in drawing in the dirt. They tried one more year, but his heart just couldn't go there. He tried to play basketball — twice. The coaches were nice and all, but it just wasn't his thing. Years later he did find a sport that he had the heart for and that sport was track. He discovered that he actually enjoyed running and that he was pretty good at it.

The coach's recent offer for him to be scorekeeper and manager of the Varsity Boys' team was really a no-brainer for the young freshman. He knew he had a lot going for him: intelligence, enthusiasm, and character, just to name a few. He also knew that basketball was not one of his special gifts. Still, being the scorekeeping and manager just might be. He'd be part of a team.

FRESHMAN: I'd love to be the team's manager!

COACH: Glad to have you aboard.

They shook hands and the conversation was over. That night at home, the young freshman told his family that he had made the varsity basketball team. Everyone stopped what they were doing. They stared at the young freshman in disbelief. Mom, always supportive, was skeptical. She knew her son well. She didn't want him to be humiliated.

MOM: Are you sure Coach didn't mean JV?

FRESHMAN: Nope, he wants me on Varsity.

Mom looked at her son's smile and his obvious joy. She thought of her son who had played basketball or attempted to play basketball in his younger years. He was like a duck out of water, but if this was what he really wanted and if coach really wanted him...

MOM: Well, we'll have to get shoes and…

The young freshman laughed out loud.

FRESHMAN: I'm manager and scorekeeper, Mom. My basketball skills are in my head, not my feet and arms.

MOM: I'd say your skills are in your heart.

# Vacations & Ventures

There's no fun like vacation fun!

# Coffee Detour

There's nothing like the excitement
of getting in your car for a family vacation.
The bags are packed and the plan is set
two weeks of traveling in unknown locations.

Oh, the thrill of seeing what you've never seen.
The sheer adrenaline that flows inside of you.
When you think that you'll soon be standing
in places where heroes once walked through.

The kids sit obediently in their designated spots;
shoes off, comfy clothes, heads lost in phones.
It doesn't take long for calm to be interrupted
with screams and pushes and constant groans.

Threats from mom are of no avail.
On the verge of an emotional crises
she hands out her sternest warning yet.
The next to complain loses their devices.

With the thought of no connection to friends,
the kids decide to chill for a while.
They settle back down in their traveling mode,
so hard to believe they've only gone fifty miles.

The hum of the engine calms Dad's disposition.
The hush is a break from the chaos of the day.
The lull and motion rock the family to sleep.
In time all but Dad are snoozing away.

Soon signs for restrooms are calling his name.
Stopping is sure to put an end to the peace.
Dad veers off the road really having no choice.
Three cups of coffee are demanding release.

# Ghost Town

I will never forget my family's visit to Ghost Town. It was an exciting and impromptu stop. It wasn't on the itinerary, but it was by far one of the best times we had that summer. We were driving back to our rented vacation house and we saw the sign for Ghost Town. Deciding we could kill a few hours, we stopped. We ended up spending more like four hours there.

Our first stop was the town's saloon. When we walked inside we saw people dressed in costumes dated back to the late 1800s. Some of us sat at the table, but my dad, uncle, and grandpa sat at the bar. The bartender told stories of ghosts that haunt the saloon at night. Us kids were too scared to listen but too curious not to. We laughed at the stories but deep down inside we were starting to feel a little creepy. My brother and cousin were scared, so Mom, my aunt, and Mimi took them out of the saloon. My sister and I stayed and listened to the whole story. I kind of wished I hadn't. The stories were etched in my brain.

Later, we went to the jailhouse, the general store, and the blacksmith. Walking down Main Street's dirt road had my mind imagining what it would be like to have lived in the Old West. This had me thinking back to the ghost stories that the bartender had told at the saloon. I kept close to Dad.

At the end of the town was a museum and a house the tour guides called a Gravity House. The house was supposedly built on a portal where gravity goes haywire. It sounded like fun and I needed a fun distraction from ghosts.

The first thing we noticed was that it was difficult to stand up. Nothing was even and not as it seemed. The mirrors that surrounded us distorted our views and it looked like aliens were staring back at us. I was once again reminded of the ghosts from the saloon. Could they have escaped and come to the Gravity House?

It took all of our energy just to walk. We were falling and picking ourselves up after every step. It was fun and annoying at the same time. Halfway through the house, we noticed that Mimi was having a more difficult time standing up than the rest of us. She kept falling and couldn't manage to ever keep her balance. My mom and aunt were trying to help her, but every time they tried, they would fall, too. We were beginning to think that Mimi would be stuck in the Gravity House forever. Even my dad, my uncle, and my grandpa couldn't help her.

She was laughing and crying at the same time. Her legs looked shorter than usual like she was crawling. Wait! She was crawling. That was the only way she could move. She would crawl and laugh and crawl some more. Finally, she made it halfway. Everyone was laughing and cheering her on. I know I shouldn't have laughed but she looked so funny!

When everyone was safe and sound and we were in the car riding back to our vacation rental, we were still laughing about Mimi in the Gravity House. It had been a great day, maybe the best one on our vacation. The ghost stories in my head no longer haunted me. I guess you could say that Mimi laughed the ghosts right out of me.

# The Fonzie Look

After a day of fun on the slides and in the pools at a renowned waterpark, it was time for a relaxing evening of pizza and later the arcade. Grandpa and Grandma were sharing a few vacation days with their four grandsons. Keeping up with them at a waterpark was exhausting, but rewarding. Each grandchild's individual personality brought their grandparents great joy. They loved nothing more than spending quality time with their grandchildren.

The three older grandsons were at the age (teens) where they were almost too cool for the youngest grandson. With a seven-year age gap, it was easy to understand how the older boys might get frustrated having a younger boy tagging along in their fun. What they failed to realize was just how much the littlest one looked up to them. In his eyes, they were tops and he wanted to be just like them.

After swimming all day, the boys showered and got dressed. It was fun to watch the older boys primp about, discussing how sharp they looked and how hot their hair looked. In the mix of their conversation, they got around to talking about girls — a topic their grandparents weren't used to hearing from them. They typically talked about sports, video games, and smack about

other people. Girls were not a topic they
generally discussed openly about in front of
adults. In truth, they were so caught up with
themselves, they forgot that grownups were
around.

After primping for a good while, using half a can
of hairspray, and a generous amount of cologne,
the three teenagers were ready to head on down
to the arcade. The youngest grandson wasn't
close to being ready. The teenagers were anxious
and wanted to go without him. Grandpa gave the
boys the okay to go but assured them that they
would be spending time with the little one once
he got to the arcade. This seemed to satisfy
them. The three left the room with Grandpa.
Grandma stayed back with the youngest
grandson.

She watched him pick out his clothes, noting that
they were very similar to the other boys' clothes,
button-up shirts, and blue jeans. After dressing,
he took a generous amount of mousse and
rubbed it in his hair. When he had it combed just
so, smooth on the sides and spiked on the top, he
sprayed it. He slapped his face with his brother's
cologne and gave himself a once over. Then, he
did the cutest thing. He gave himself two thumbs
up into the mirror and smiled from ear to ear.

"Aaaaay," he said to himself, mimicking The Fonz, a famous sitcom character from the popular syndicated sitcom *Happy Days*.

Like Fonzie, the littlest grandson was self-assured. Grandma had to laugh out loud. Oh, but he did look handsome! She wasn't going to argue with such perfection. He told her that he was ready to go. She picked up her purse and smiled lovingly at him. She knew one thing, she would have the coolest, most handsome date in the arcade.

As they walked down to the arcade, she couldn't stop smiling at her little man. She kept picturing a jukebox in her head and the song she heard was a familiar tune. She started humming it. The lyrics flowed true within her spirit. These days were truly her happy days.

# About the Author

**B. Ellen Gardner** is a graduate of Texas Woman's University. She has taught school for almost thirty years and has been writing for as long as she can remember. Her novels include a variety of genres: Historical, Contemporary, and Mystery, along with her poetry. When Ellen isn't writing or teaching, she enjoys the love of her husband, children, and grandchildren.

Made in the USA
Las Vegas, NV
11 February 2021